T0104661

12 STEPS TO
HEALTH,

Wealth,
AND JOY

A GUIDE TO LIVING WELL

MICHELLE FARIAS

Order this book online at www.trafford.com
or email orders@trafford.com

Most Trafford titles are also available at major online book retailers.

Printed in the United States of America.

ISBN: 978-1-4669-8692-3 (sc)
ISBN: 978-1-4669-8662-6 (e)

Trafford rev. 03/20/2013

 www.trafford.com

North America & international
toll-free: 1 888 232 4444 (USA & Canada)
phone: 250 383 6864 ♦ fax: 812 355 4082

CONTENTS

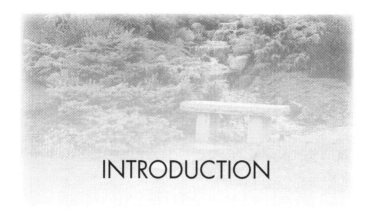

INTRODUCTION

*L*ife is meant to be fun. This is an amazing time to be alive in an environment rich with opportunity. We are here to explore our environment and we get to choose the kind of life we want to live. Joy and excitement should be a part of your daily life. Struggles and disappointments are inevitable, but they are not permanent. The challenges we face are simply opportunities for growth and they allow us to create the incredible lives we came here to experience. Your life is constantly evolving. It might be easy to feel like you are stuck in life, but you are never stuck. If you don't feel like your life is changing, it simply means that you are repeating the same habits and thoughts that keep you in the same situation. When you change your thoughts and habits, you change your life.

You have within you everything you need to create the life you want. You don't need to spend a lot of money on experts or material goods to change your life. You know best what is right for you, and you have within you the guidance that will give you direction. Trust in yourself and know that you already have everything you need for success and joy.

12 Steps to Health, Wealth and Joy consists of simple lessons that will help you tap into your inner guidance and create an amazing life. Each lesson targets an area of life that might be challenging, and each is followed by activities that will help propel you toward a different experience. The activities might appear simplistic, but they are powerful. Some will feel good to practice while others will be more of a struggle. Find what works for you, and then practice those strategies regularly. The more you practice and commit to change, the bigger your life will become.

Although it might be tempting to read through this book quickly, pace yourself and work through one lesson a week. Read and reread each one several times during the week while you practice the accompanying activity. Give yourself time to digest the information and feel comfortable with the activities.

Enjoy these lessons, and allow yourself to uncover the potential of your life. Feeling good and enjoying life is exhilarating. Let go of the reins and watch your life unfold. This is an exciting time to be alive.

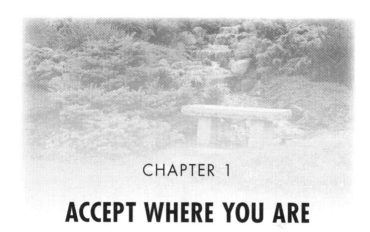

CHAPTER 1

ACCEPT WHERE YOU ARE

*Y*ou are where you are. Accept it. It's not good or bad. It's just where you are. It doesn't matter where that is. Make peace with where you are and stop struggling against it. Make this your mantra:

I am where I am, and it's okay.
I can't pay my bills, and it's okay.
I weigh one hundred pounds more than I'd like, and it's okay.
I'm lonely, and it's okay.
I don't love my partner, and it's okay.

This is where you are, and there is nothing wrong with where you are. Do not fight against it any longer. Accept it. Be at peace with it. Relax in it. Embrace it. Breathe it. You can't be in a different place at this moment, *but* the next moments can change, depending on your thoughts.

You have within you the power to change where you are and live the life you desire. Feel the confidence that comes from knowing that this is all temporary, and you can deliberately make big or little changes at any time. Change is easy to accomplish, and the process for creating change is powerful.

You probably have things you want to change that you believe will make you happy. The paradox is that until you get happy, you can't receive those things that you believe will make you happy. Real happiness doesn't come from the outside through people, places or things. Happiness is internal—it's within you. The stuff outside of you can make it easier to feel happy, but if your happiness depends on external factors, you will live a rollercoaster life.

Ultimately, it's up to you to feel good. The tricky part is that people tend to attract things that match how they habitually feel. So, if you're happy, you will attract more happiness. If you're struggling, worried, or frustrated, you will attract more of the same.

You have to feel good where you are before you can hope to achieve more happiness. If you can't feel good, then at least feel better. Just reach for a better mindset. Let's look at how a stream of thoughts can move a person from feeling bad to feeling better.

<u>Anger</u>
"My ex forgot to call our son on his birthday again! I can't believe this. It hurts our son so much to be forgotten, and it's just a mean thing to do. I'm furious!"

From here, find a thought that brings you some relief from anger—possibly frustration.

Frustration

"I don't wish for a horrible thing to happen to my ex, but I wish my son would have at least received a phone call because it feels good for him."

The actual emotion doesn't matter. Feeling better by thinking a thought that brings relief will help guide you toward feeling good. Eventually, you might be able to approach the situation in a positive manner.

Empowerment

"My ex always forgets my son's birthday, but I have taught my son that even though a phone call would feel good, he is loved and he can feel good in other ways as well."

This feeling of empowerment brings relief from the tension in your stomach. You will create a fabulous life when you habitually look for ways to feel better, and this is a life of which you are worthy. Feeling good is simply about thinking thoughts that bring relief to you *now*.

Right now, you are worthy of all that you desire simply because you are here. You don't have to prove yourself. You showed up for this life and that gives you all of the worthiness you need to live a life of love and joy. Your value or worthiness is not dependent upon what you have accumulated or what you have accomplished. Awards, promotions, raises, money, or acknowledgements don't make you worthy. You are worthy just because you are. It doesn't matter what anyone told you growing up, or what anyone is telling you at this moment. Someone outside of you cannot deem you worthy or unworthy. Someone outside of you does not hold the key to your happiness. Your worthiness is not in question. It just is. You are powerful, valuable, and worthy. Claim it.

Right now, in your worthiness, you are a creator. You are the creator of your own experience—a creator of things others have not even thought to create. You create with every thought. Embrace this power and enjoy it. Your life will be as good as you allow it to be.

You are a creator in the present—not the past. You don't have to go back and undo anything that has been done. You don't have to feel guilty or have regrets about the past. All you have to do is embrace where you are and move forward. The past has been valuable for you because you have learned what you do and do not prefer based on past experiences. The contrast that you have experienced clarifies what you want for yourself. You have a clearer picture of what makes you happy based on your previous experiences. Yet, you are not bound by the past. You are free from it. You don't have to live with regrets and guilt. You are free to create your life in a way that will bring you fulfillment and joy.

Accept where you are. Make peace with you in this moment. Know the power you have to change the next moment. Buckle up. This is quite a ride!

Activity: Conscious Breathing

We often become frustrated with our place in life. It seems as if nothing is ever going to change, and we can feel hopeless. Accepting where you are does not mean that you stop wanting new things; it means that you are soothing the struggle you feel with your *now*. The best way for you to soothe yourself in the moment is through conscious breathing.

- Find a quiet place to sit where you won't be disturbed.
- Sit comfortably and close your eyes.
- Notice your breathing as your breath enters and leaves your body.
- Breathe in and feel the air fill your lungs and expand into your stomach.
- Slowly release the air through your mouth and relax your stomach.
- Breathe in again and release.
- Feel your body relax and your mind rest.
- Breathe in again and release.
- If thoughts come into your mind, release them as you exhale.
- Continue this exercise for several minutes.

Practice conscious breathing several times a day whenever you are feeling anxious or unsettled. You will be able to relax and stay in the moment which will help you be at peace.

CHAPTER 2

TAKE RESPONSIBILITY FOR YOUR LIFE

*Y*ou create your life. Many people have grown accustomed to holding others responsible for their lives. Unstable parents, uncaring teachers, unethical governments, crazy neighbors, irresponsible friends, and unappreciative children have all been blamed for the reality of people's lives. It is true that there are many encounters with individuals and entities that would like to influence your life, but ultimately you are the one who is creating it. You are the one thinking the thoughts and making the decisions that are guiding your life.

Taking responsibility for your life gives you ultimate freedom. You are no longer at the mercy of others' actions. You no longer have to just react to what is going on around you because you become the guiding force in your life. When you take responsibility for your decisions, your beliefs, and your actions, you are free to create the life you desire. You no longer have to live in fear or spend your life waiting for something to happen. You make it happen—all of it.

Your thoughts and actions in the present moment are creating your future. Chronic thoughts of hope, enthusiasm and joy will create a fun and enriching life. Chronic thoughts of worry, anxiety, dread and anger will create a difficult and uncomfortable life. Being aware of your dominant thoughts and their resulting emotions is a valuable tool for changing your life.

Accepting responsibility for your life does not mean assigning blame to a situation. Your life is what it is; it was what it was. Making peace with yourself and those who have influenced you will empower you to take control and consciously create the life you desire.

You have complete control over what happens to you. Accepting this idea is the key to changing your life. When you blame others or external conditions for what is happening to you, you are a victim and powerless to make changes in your life. It is understandable to be angry with others who treated you badly and to blame them for your experience. These feelings are important to acknowledge. Yet it is even more important to release them and find relief in other thoughts. Look at the different emotional effects of these statements.

Blame

"My parents treated me badly and now I can't maintain a stable relationship."

Disappointment
"I wish my parents had been able to spend more time with me. It would have made my life easier."

Pessimism
"I guess all parents let down their kids. Mine were no different."

Hopeful
"It doesn't really matter now what my parents were like. I am an adult, and I can create a better life for myself."

Empowering
"I have all I need to create the life I want right now."

Releasing the negative thoughts is about helping YOU feel better—nothing else. Finding positivity amongst your thoughts will help empower you to take control of your life.

You take yourself wherever you go. It doesn't matter how many times you change relationships, jobs, or homes. The one constant is you. If you don't take responsibility for your life and make an effort to be more positive, you will continue to experience the negative situations that you are trying to escape. Allow yourself to relax and trust that all you want will come to you. Worry and fear only keep the good stuff away. Trust in your well-being and accept responsibility for your life. Find the freedom through this trust and acceptance and become empowered. You create your life. You are responsible for your life. You can change your life. You can—and you will—achieve all of your desires, one thought at a time.

Activity: Feel the Change

You've taken responsibility for your life, and you know you have the power to create change. Maybe it doesn't seem feasible for the change you want to happen right now, but it could happen in the near future. Spend some time throughout your day imagining how you would feel if you made one change—any change in your life. Look for situations where a change would be enjoyable. Say to yourself, "I would enjoy . . ."

- "I would enjoy a new house."
- "I would enjoy a loving partner."
- "I would enjoy living on the beach."
- "I would enjoy getting more sleep."
- "I would enjoy losing ten pounds."

It doesn't matter what you choose to imagine; the only thing that matters is how you feel. Make your statement and really think about how the change would feel to you. Allow the good feelings to flow through you as you visualize the change you want to live. Imagine the specifics of your desire and enjoy the experience as the details unfold. Don't allow doubt or "reality" to invade your imagination. This is purely your desire. Enjoy this feeling. Do this activity several times a day and watch as your imagination comes to life.

CHAPTER 3

YOUR EMOTIONS

Our lives are lived through our emotions. We generally try to do what feels good and avoid what feels bad. Our emotions are our GPS system, guiding our decisions. If we pay attention to them, we can know what is right for us and what we should avoid. If we ignore our emotions and listen to others' advice or do what we think others want us to do, we can get off track and live a less-fulfilling life. Our emotions do not judge us or trick us; they simply let us know if we are moving toward or away from our desires.

Your environment provides ample opportunity for your emotions to speak to you. When you see something you don't like, your emotions tell you what it is you would prefer. Tuning in to your emotions will give you the powerful guidance you need to make choices that are right for you.

These choices may not be right for your parents, your friends, or your boss, but they are right for you. There are a wide variety of preferences, beliefs and lifestyles. You don't get to choose for others and they don't get to choose for you. Your focus is to pay attention to what feels right for you by listening to your emotions.

You basically have two categories of emotions—one that feels good and one that feels bad. Although there are a wide variety of emotions in each category, your life is guided by the positive and negative emotions you experience. Good feels good. Bad feels bad. Strive for the good-feeling thoughts.

Pay attention to the emotions that accompany your thoughts. The more positive your emotions are, the more joy you will experience. You feel pure joy and love when you look at an image of beauty or innocence. You are in a state of appreciation; there is no resistance, worry or fear. You are in the presence of everything that is good. Look at a child or the sunset and experience this feeling. It is a moment of pure joy. Life *can* be about feeling good if you focus on thoughts that feel good.

Positive emotions create wanted conditions; negative emotions create unwanted conditions. The thoughts you are thinking now are paving the way for your future experience. Your goal is to simply find those thoughts that bring some relief to what you are feeling right now.

This process works for any subject that evokes feelings. You might worry about having a heart attack some day because your mother had a heart attack, and you have high cholesterol. To add to your worry, your doctor has warned you that you are a prime candidate for a heart attack. You might feel physically fine, but the signs and warnings are shouting at you that you will one day have a heart attack. Your worry has evolved into panic, and you start imagining being wheeled into the emergency room with chest pains. This experience is becoming too real for you, and you are now maintaining chronic negative thoughts about your health and potential heart attack.

The problem with this scenario is that your heart is fine. Your body is healthy. You are living a life of well-being, but you are paying attention to what people outside of you are telling you about your body. You begin visualizing having a heart attack. Just stop! This is the prime opportunity to start reaching for thoughts that bring relief.

Look at your thoughts. Instead of thinking, *"My mother had a heart attack, so I probably will also,"* you can think, *"My mother had a heart attack, but I am healthy. I know a lot more about taking care of myself, and I feel good. My body and experiences are independent from my mother's, and I intend to stay healthy."* Your thoughts about the wellness of your body are far more powerful than any tests, research or lifestyle plan. Your thoughts can keep your body healthy, or they can create illness. The choice is yours.

Appreciate the moments when you have negative feelings because these are clear indicators that you are not allowing your joyful desires and well-being to come to you. Embrace the negative feelings for showing you where you are on your journey, and then reach for a thought that brings relief.

Whether you are thinking about a past experience, a present situation, or a future possibility, choose thoughts that feel good. It doesn't matter if the subject is large or small, reaching for relief will always lead you to a life of joy. You don't need to be intense about every thought you think. Just relax as you begin to practice thinking in more positive ways.

All that matters is that you feel good most of the time. Something might happen to anger you, and you might be very justified in your anger. You may have been treated unfairly, and you want to be mad. If feeling angry feels good at the moment, then feel angry. But, don't stay focused on your anger. Don't rehash the story to others of how you were treated unfairly. Don't spend the next days or weeks remembering how you were treated. Instead, think in a way that brings relief from the anger, and continue to do so until you feel better. Feeling good most of the time will help you to create the changes you want in your life. Choosing to feel bad most of the time can keep you stuck. As always, the choice is yours.

There will be times when you want to be negative. It just feels good at the moment to complain about someone or something. But limit your complaining. When you complain or focus on worry, doubt, or fear, you will find your life filled with negativity. Negativity draws the attention to what is lacking in your life. Positive feelings enhance abundance.

Focus on appreciation and make endless lists of what you love and appreciate. You may not see evidence of change in your life right away, but you will begin to change immediately, and then everything else will follow. Immerse yourself in good thoughts and activities, and you will find easy access to more good thoughts and activities. Doors will open up for you, people will come into your life, and things will just get easier. Feeling good is the only action you need to change your life.

Training yourself to pay attention to your emotions takes practice. Be patient with yourself. There is no hurry, and you can't do it wrong. One good thought chosen over one bad thought is progress. Be proud of yourself for the successes you notice throughout the day. You are changing a lifetime of thinking habits, so this might take time. However, once you do so, you will soon find yourself experiencing more joy than you knew existed.

Activity: Your Emotions
Changing patterns of thought and your emotional response takes practice. You have to remember to focus on thoughts that feel good and make this a habit. To help you change your thought habits, put reminders to be positive around your home, work place and car. Brainstorm and make a word list, or cut out pictures of all of the things that feel good such as family, friends, hobbies, and vacation spots. (Images are powerful influences on the brain since they are rich with detail.) Put these reminders everywhere, and make an intention to notice them throughout the day.

When you notice them, stop and really appreciate why you like what you are reading or seeing. When you do this enough, you will begin to find reasons to feel good on your own, and you will notice a positive shift in your feelings throughout the day.

CHAPTER 4

ALLOW CLARITY FOR YOUR LIFE TO COME THROUGH

any people spend their lives searching for their purpose. Our purpose is simply to live the life we choose to live and feel good about it.

When you make your choices based on joy, your life is a success.

Knowing what is right for you and what path to take is easy. Your pursuit is joy, and your emotions will indicate whether you are following joy or despair.

Your desires are what you believe will bring you joy. Desire is the exciting feeling of new possibilities that are available for you. Desire is free and light.

Your desire should not feel so big that you do not believe it will happen. You have to believe in the possibility of your desire before it can come to you. You have to expect it to manifest—the power of expectation. What you believe and thus expect *will* show up in your life. If you expect for your partner to treat you badly, you will attract partners who will treat you badly. If you expect to get a wonderful job, you will find one that is a perfect fit. Expectation is a powerful force.

Your desire should feel easy. It should be the next logical step. I might be currently living in a 1,500 square foot house and have a desire to live in a 10,000 square foot mansion. Yet this would probably be too big of a step. However, moving into a 4000 square foot home feels more reasonable, and so this is the next logical step in my desire to expand my home.

The ultimate point of clarity for you is to discern what desire brings you joy and then believe it is possible. When you believe what you want is possible, you allow your desire to come to you. When you do not believe your desire is possible, you resist its manifestation in your life. Clarity means simply to desire, believe, and enjoy.

Tell your life story the way you want it to be. Tell short segments of your ideal life story many times throughout the day. Ignore your present reality, and talk about your ideal life. Cut out pictures. Draw sketches. Gather together your ideal life. Talk about your career, relationships, health, body, finances, hobbies, recreation and anything that brings you joy. Repeat, repeat, repeat. Do not limit your desires. When you limit your desires or discount them as impossible, you limit your life. The possibilities—no matter how outrageous—are possible.

The resources needed to accomplish your desires will come to you when you allow yourself to believe. You don't have worry about the how, when, or who of your desires. If you get caught up in the struggle of trying to figure out *how* to make something happen, you will create struggle. You have no way of knowing all of the avenues and people from which your desires can come. You only have to know this will happen. The stronger your expectancy, the quicker your desires will manifest.

You are unlimited. Life flows easily in and out of your experience. When you notice something you do not want, avoid analyzing it or talking about it. Just ignore it. You are provided with contrast to help you discern that which you do want. Simply look away from what you do not want and toward what you do want.

Resist the temptation to replay negative events of your life, trying to figure out what went wrong. What went wrong does not matter as much as feeling good and discovering what you want. So what do you want? Just start where you are—now—and find what feels good, what feels like relief.

Your positive, good-feeling emotions let you know that you are aligning yourself with your desires. These emotions indicate that you are on the right path. This is all you need to find your way. While you hold consistently to these positive, good-feeling thoughts, your desires will make their way to you.

No one can control your thoughts, and that is where freedom begins. Freedom is at the core of your desires. You don't create freedom through action. Action is just a small part of your creation. You create your freedom through thoughts. Think your thoughts first, and then you will inspire action. If you try to skip the thought element, your action will be difficult, draining, and often unsuccessful.

Your thoughts do the majority of the work. The inspired action that follows will then be easy. You are always thinking—your mind is always working. Your task is to direct your flow of thoughts to the positive side rather than the negative side. Lazy thinking allows your mind to endlessly wander and to only think about what you see in front of you. Purposeful thinking requires that you notice your thoughts and purposely direct them.

Seeking joy in your thoughts will provide clarity in your life that you can be, do or have whatever you desire. This is your life's purpose.

Activity: Insightful Drawing
Drawing is a method used to gain insight into your present life and provide the answers that seem to elude you. Do this activity in a quiet place where you won't be interrupted to get the most benefit. You will need a sheet of paper and something with which to draw.

- Take a few moments to breathe and notice your breath entering and leaving your body. When you feel relaxed, you may begin.
- Take a sheet of paper and divide it into three equal parts. On the first section, draw how you see

yourself now. Don't worry about being artistic—just draw what comes to mind. Take time with your drawing, but don't get too stuck on the details. The overall image is what matters.

- On the second section, draw what your biggest problem is right now. It doesn't matter if the problem feels huge or trivial. Draw whatever comes to mind.

- On the third section, draw what it looks like when your problem is solved. What images come to you when you think about your biggest problem getting resolved? Spend a few moments drawing this.

- When you are finished, put down your pen or pencil and look at your drawings. What do you see in the first drawing? How did you depict yourself? Are you big or little? Are other people with you? What stands out for you in your drawing? What does this drawing say about your "now" experience?

- Look at your second drawing. How do you feel when you look at this drawing? What does this say about you and your problem?

- Look at your third drawing. What stands out for you in the third drawing? Do you look different here than in the first one? What changes do you see? Do you see any solutions to your problem when you look at all three drawings?

Drawings can provide insight into those issues with which you are struggling. Make peace with where you are at this moment, and utilize tools to help you find relief right now so that you see solutions as they are presented to you. If you liked this activity, use it when you are feeling stuck or unsure. It can provide you with valuable insight.

CHAPTER 5

LIVE FROM THE INSIDE OUT

ll of your actions can be guided by your emotions. Tuning into how something feels is the best indicator of whether or not you are connected with you. There is not one thing, institution, or person outside of you that can guide you better than yourself. No one can make a decision for you that is better than any decision you make for yourself. Your decisions should be based on how they feel—selfishly feel—to you.

Inspiration to action can't come from trying to please others. When you live for the approval of others rather than your own fulfillment, you become disconnected. What are you doing to please others? Have you altered your career, relationships, goals, desires, finances, conversation, parenting, hobbies, dress or appearance to please others? What part of you do you minimize so others will approve? Your primary goal is to feel good, and when you push down the good feelings so that others will accept you or your actions, you are pinching yourself off from who you are truly meant to be and your right to happiness.

What would it feel like to not worry about what other people think? What kind of day would you have if you dressed, ate, interacted, made choices, and believed without worrying about what others thought of you? How would it be to not have the constant critical voice in your head judging you? What gives you the right to make your own decisions and live life the way it pleases you? You have this right simply because you exist. You are worthy of this right.

Diversity abounds in society, and no two people can agree on what is right for the other. Different backgrounds, experiences, lifestyles, preferences, and beliefs are abundant in society, and it is meant to be this way. This is how the world expands. Diversity creates contrast, so you get to choose what is right for you. You don't have to allow others to choose for you and you don't get to choose for them. This is what makes living in this time so amazing.

You receive feedback on how to live your life from many outside sources. In addition to friends and family giving you advice, the media will offer numerous stories and research studies to help guide your life. Statistics about health concerns, financial problems, world events, and relationship issues are given to help you make decisions for your life. Yet these statistics are about other people. They are not about your specific life. Everyone in your neighborhood could be experiencing a foreclosure, but that does not mean you will also. Every paternal relative could have colon cancer, but that does not mean you will. Statistics do not tell you about your life, yet if you give them enough attention, you can reinforce the statistic, which will then reinforce your belief in them. The only guide you need on how to live your life is your emotions.

How do you feel when others comment on your life or decisions? Do you feel good, or do you find yourself feeling worried, anxious or depressed? Begin to visualize how it would feel to ignore others' advice about your life. What would happen if you immediately discounted any advice, criticism, or warning? Simply say this to yourself:

"I have the best guidance in the world through my emotions, and there is nothing anyone can say that will lead me to more health and well-being than my own feelings."

People who truly want you to be happy will leave you to live your own life. Those who don't care about your happiness will not approve of you, regardless of what you do, so you can stop trying to please them. When you focus on trying to please others, you lose yourself. The only person you can please is you. As you practice pleasing yourself, you will become an inspiration to others who want to feel good.

You will gain confidence by making choices based on your emotions rather than depending on outside forces. You will soon become very comfortable trusting yourself, and the opinions of others will go unnoticed. When you spend time clarifying what you want, visualizing it, feeling good about it, and then allowing the right moment for your choices to unfold, you can feel comfortable with your choices even if someone else is bothered by your decisions. You will, then, be able to make choices without justifying them to others because you know the choices you made are the right ones for you. Those around you will either come to appreciate you or they will move on.

Live your life from the inside out. Look for clarity through your emotions. Understand that other well-meaning people will try to influence your choices, but it is ultimately up to you to choose what is best for you. No one else can do it but you.

Activity: Reflection Circle

We receive hundreds of messages each day—both positive and negative—from other people and from ourselves. These messages affect how we feel about ourselves, and they impact our daily decisions. The reflection circle will help increase your awareness of these messages and give you tools to counter them.

- You will need a sheet a paper, a pencil, and markers or crayons.
- Using a round object as a guide, draw a large circle on your paper.
- In the middle of the circle, draw an image that represents you.
- Outside of the circle write words or draw images that represent the frequent negative messages you

get from others or you tell yourself. Write/draw as many as you can remember.

- On the inside of the circle, write words or draw images that represent all of the positive aspects about you. Be as general or specific as you wish including positive thoughts about how your body works, your work abilities, your creativity, and your social skills.

- When you have finished, look at your circle. Was it harder to think of things for the outside of the circle or the inside? Which part has more words/images? What does this circle drawing tell you about how you let outside messages affect you?

Keep your circle somewhere where you will notice it. Use it as a reminder that others do not get to define who you are and what is right for you. What feels right to one person does not feel right to another, but that is what creates a diverse society. Trust in your instincts for your life and do what feels good. When you listen to your inner being, you can never get it wrong.

CHAPTER 6

GETTING WHAT YOU WANT

*D*esires are endless. Ask children if all of their desires have been fulfilled, and they will tell you, "No. I want more!" You will continually have desires because you are constantly evolving. Every day brings a new you and a new desire.

We are co-creating in this world, and everyone now and in the future benefits from your desires. Feel eager and excited at the creation of all of your wants. Life, though, is not only about enjoying your creation. The vitality of life comes from experiencing the joy and excitement that comes from anticipating the arrival of your creations. This is where the real energy is. Think about the holiday season. Anticipation begins to build in summer with *Christmas in July* sales. After Labor Day, the decorations appear in the stores, and children begin making Christmas lists. Many people start shopping for gifts after Halloween, and the excitement is full-blown after Thanksgiving. Anticipation is what creates the energy during the season, and many people feel joy as they look forward to Christmas Day. Yet once the actual day arrives, it flies by quickly.

This is how life works. You create a desire, you are excited about its manifestation (where the true energy lies), and then when it appears, you enjoy it and move on to the next desire. So, enjoy the excitement of waiting. It is not really the actual thing or event that is bringing you joy. It is the fun you are having waiting for its arrival. You imagine it; you are thrilled with the idea of it; you look forward to it. This is the zest of life.

All things are possible. If you think it, it can happen. You can be, do, or have whatever you want. You create your life through the power of your focus, and you allow good things to enter your life through your feelings. Your focus involves what you think, speak, write, listen to, imagine, remember, and observe. What you choose to focus on affects your thoughts and feelings which allow or disallow your desires. This creates your life.

Many people argue that they are focusing on what they want and feeling good about it, but what they want is still not manifesting. Often, though, people are focusing on the lack of what they want.

- *"I want more money because I can't pay my bills,"* focuses on lack. Compare this to: *"I want more money because I will feel good having financial freedom."* This focuses on abundance.

- *"I want a relationship because I am lonely,"* focuses on lack. Compare this to: *"I want a relationship because it will be fun to share experiences with another,"* which focuses on abundance.

The message in the thoughts you create is what you are drawing into your experience. The key is to look at your feelings when you are creating. If your thoughts make you feel good (excitement, happiness, eagerness), then you are focusing on abundance. When you feel negative (doubtful, discouraged, pessimistic), then your thought is one of lack, and you attract the opposite of what you want. Your emotions will show you if you are focusing on abundance or lack. Your primary goal each day is to feel good. When you feel good, all good things come to you.

Impatience will keep your desires away. Frustration of how long it is taking to enjoy your desires will keep your desires away. You don't start an educational program and then quit after the completing the first course because you are frustrated that you haven't finished the program. You accept that it will take a while to complete the program and graduate. The process of graduating means taking time to learn what is being taught and practicing the new ideas before you are ready for your diploma. You enter the program with a powerful expectation that you will finish and obtain your degree. You have patience and appreciation for the process. In due time, you will graduate. Your desires will come to you in the same way. Everything occurs in perfect time, and when you are aligned with *you* and feeling good, you draw your desire to you.

Your desires come from wanting to feel good. *"If I had more money, I would feel good." "If I lost weight, I would feel good." "If I met my soul mate, I would feel good."* These beliefs are understandable, but you cannot attract something that feels good from a place that feels bad. You must feel good to attract what you want.

- If you want to meet your soul mate, then get to a place where you are habitually feeling good about yourself and you will attract someone with the same experience. The alternative is to feel lonely and desperate, and you will attract someone who is lonely and desperate.
- If you want to lose weight, then behave as if you were thinner. Move more, eat for nutrition and feel good in your body. If you continue the behavior of being lethargic and feeling fat, then you are more likely to stay overweight.

The bottom line is you have to feel good first. You have to feel so good that it won't matter if what you want never comes because you are already joyful. Yet when you are feeling that good, the stuff you want will come, and it will be even more amazing.

Life is supposed to be fun. You have to expect it to be fun. When something becomes a struggle, just relax and find something fun to do. Expect good things to happen.

Just as you know the store will be there when you go shopping, you must have that same expectancy for your desires. You expect your place of work to be there when you arrive; you expect your home to be there when you return home; you expect your desires to manifest.

Your belief has to be so strong that you already feel what you want has arrived. You want to feel so good that when your desires appear, you might not even notice them. If you are not feeling good and your desire shows up, you will miss the opportunity you have been waiting for because you are not at a point where you can see it. My husband and I grew up within five miles of each other. We shopped at the same stores, went to the same church and even knew some of the same people. Yet, it wasn't until we were both at a point where we were happy in our lives (in our thirties) that we met. We were engaged three months later. Get happy and have fun with what appears.

If you have been practicing negative thoughts for a while, you might have to take some time to adjust your thoughts to ones that are more open. Habits can quickly change. Yet if you do not change your thoughts first, changing habits will feel impossible. When you get into the habit of feeling good, you will continue to feel good. It becomes a part of you, and your desires appear more easily. Some people get discouraged because what they wanted did not appear as specifically as they imagined. Their desired soul mate did not show up six feet tall. It is not the specifics that create the good feelings. It is the essence of the person or situation that feels good, and feeling good is the true desire.

Tell your good-feeling story many times throughout the day. Tell the story of how you intend for your life to be. Tell your story with words, images, pictures, visualizations, in paintings, writings, and more. Start imagining your life as you want it to be, and have fun with it. Throughout your day, look for reasons to laugh, feel good and have fun. Be proactive creating a day where it is easy to feel good.

Activity: Guided Imagery
Imagery is the language of our unrestricted mind. Utilizing our senses of touch, sight, smell, hearing and taste, we can create whatever movie we wish in our minds. We can take any subject that we want to change and create the change in our mind. This is easy and relaxing. Imagery also is exciting as you see the change you want to create.

- Find a quiet place where you won't be disturbed.
- Sit comfortably and allow yourself to relax.
- Practice your breathing so that you feel the air move in through your nose, sense it fill your body, and release it through your mouth.
- Breathe like this for a few minutes
- When you are ready, see yourself in a current situation that you want to change. Notice your appearance, the sounds around you, and any smells that surface. Look around and see what surrounds you. Feel yourself in your scene.

- When you feel you are part of the scene, see yourself making a change. It does not matter what it is—or even if it seems realistic. Just have fun with the image you are creating. As you watch the change occur, notice how your body is responding. Do you feel excited? Are the sights, sounds and smells changing? Is there something you can touch? Immerse yourself in the change.

- Spend time in your new experience. Notice how others who enter your image respond to you. Feel good about where you are and enjoy. Continue breathing and focusing on how good it feels to experience the change you are creating.

- After at least fifteen minutes of experiencing your imagery, slowly bring your awareness back to the present. Open your eyes when you are ready. Remember the feeling you imagined where you created a change that felt good.

- Continue practicing imagery a few times a week. The more you create a positive change in your mind, the quicker and easier it will be to see the change manifest in your "real" world.

CHAPTER 7

STRUGGLING AGAINST WHAT YOU WANT

*N*o matter how big your dreams are, they will not come if you do not believe and allow them. You disallow your dreams through struggle. Struggle comes in the form of negative thoughts.

"I'm not good enough."
"I don't have enough money or time."
"I don't know the right people."
"I'm not smart enough."
"No one has ever done this before so how can I do it?"
"This is more than I can handle."
"I don't know how to make this work."
"My parents would not approve."
"This would take too long."
"People will laugh at me."
"I don't think it will work."

Negative thoughts create struggle. Positive thoughts allow. To determine where your thoughts fall, pay attention to how you feel. Thoughts that feel good are allowing, and thoughts that feel bad are creating a struggle. You can't be focused on negative and positive at the same time. Start where you are and point positive.

Struggle creates fatigue. Many people believe they are tired because they are so busy when in fact they are tired because so much of their energy is spent on struggling against their natural well-being. Every moment you spend thinking about what you do not want drains your energy. Negative emotion is a sign that you are cutting yourself off from you and who you have been created to be. Allow your well-being, and feel the surge of energy.

Struggle appears in many forms:

- Retelling a story of how you were wronged to others who are empathetic to your situation.
- Picking apart the pieces of an experience to find out what went wrong.
- Thinking thoughts that do not feel good.
- Being angry with another (justified or not).
- Analyzing a situation to find the source of the unpleasant experience.
- Focusing on lack of what you want. (i.e., *I want my kids to be better behaved because they are so embarrassing to be with in public*," or "*I wish our*

> *government would start behaving ethically because it is abusing its power.")*

- Justifying, explaining, or rationalizing your choices.
- Focusing on what you do not want.
- Hearing negative stories and allowing them to affect you.
- Trying to please others or listening to the advice of others when it conflicts with your own desires.
- Saying, "*I want it, but . . .*"
- Continuing to notice that what you want is still not here.
- Waiting for what you want to appear. (A watched pot never boils.)
- Looking at the reality of your life.
- Feeling a shortage of time, money, health, fun, and so on.
- Protesting/fighting for justice/
- Focusing on problems rather than solutions.
- Believing that something bad outside of you is causing your distress.

You will have challenges that can create temporary distress for you, but if you are habitually feeling good, you will quickly find your way back to your positive self. I know many people who habitually feel bad, and they are on the lookout for other things about which to feel bad. All they have to do is watch the news, and they can find plenty of things to add to their depression. But, if you are in the habit of feeling good and something bad happens, you work through it by focusing on positive thinking. You will soon find yourself back to joy in no time. When you allow yourself to feel good, you feel healthy, abundant, energetic, and positive. When you don't, you feel ill, poor, and fearful. Nothing outside of you creates your experience. It is all up to you to create the life you want.

Most negativity comes from feelings of being unworthy or undeserving of the good things in life. Any negative feelings you have toward yourself create struggle. Additionally, when you are negative about yourself, you are more likely to have negative feelings about the people and things around you, and you will attract negativity into your experience. Negativity attracts negativity.

Focusing on the positive aspects about yourself will bring out the positive aspects of those around you, and you will attract more positive people. If you start to feel negative about yourself, find something about you that is easier to be positive about—maybe that you are very organized or dependable. If you cannot find anything positive about yourself, find something positive in your surroundings. The point is to change your focus to feeling positive. Focus on this positive aspect about yourself or your surroundings for a few days and then allow yourself to find other things about yourself to feel positive.

Sometimes, you just cannot get to a more positive place regarding a particular issue. If you are struggling financially, it might be hard to feel good since you do not have enough money to go to the store or pay the bills. If you want to lose weight, you might struggle to feel good since you take your body with you wherever you go. A loved one may have died, and you just cannot move away from the grief that goes with missing someone. When you have a situation where you cannot find a better frame of mind, then just stop thinking about it. Put it on a shelf and focus your attention on more positive things. After a break—maybe a few days or a few weeks—return to the issue to see if you are ready to think about it in a more positive way. If not, then stop thinking about it again and take another break. Continue this until you can begin to feel better about the situation. You may be justified feeling negative about something, but this does not help you or anyone around you. You can feel right or you can feel better.

You may not be today where you want to be. Yet, it will all change in time. You have the ability to focus your thoughts and find things to appreciate wherever you are. You are constantly evolving. If you want a different experience, tell a different story. Your desires are coming to you. Feel good.

Activity: Write Your Life
Writing is a powerful tool for creating change in your life. The actual act of writing—not typing—can help you find insight and solutions to problems that seem daunting.

- Find a quiet place where you won't be disturbed. Have paper and something with which to write.

- Take a few moments to do purposeful breathing, and allow your body to relax.

- When you feel yourself relax, think about what your perfect day would be like. Where would you wake up and at what time? Will you be with anyone or by yourself? What is the weather like outside? Notice how rested and eager you are to live this day. Imagine what you will do once you get out of bed. Continue to think about what would make this day your perfect day.

- When you are ready, write down your perfect day. What did you imagine? Be as specific and detailed as possible. Include what you are wearing, who is with you, how you feel, and so on. Don't let doubt or "reality" creep into your day. Do only what feels good and brings you joy.

- If problems emerge in your perfect day, hand them to someone else to handle and continue enjoying the precise unfolding of your satisfying day.

- Keep this writing in a safe place, and read it whenever you are feeling discouraged.

- If this activity feels good, continue doing it to build confidence in your ability to create your life. It will all happen in perfect time.

CHAPTER 8

CREATING YOUR HEALTH

*Y*our body reflects your thoughts. What you are thinking and feeling has a direct impact on your body. This idea is often difficult to accept because most people don't want to believe that they caused the illness that permeates their bodies. People don't consciously attract cancer or diabetes, but the habitual thoughts we think can be a perfect match to our health conditions—both positive and negative. Chronic negative emotions combined with negative thinking about health and wellness are strong indicators that a health issue might appear in the future.

Society is inundated with information about potential health problems. The news reports the latest research on the effects of diseases, what causes diseases, and who is at-risk for contracting a disease. Commercials, magazine articles, and stories are written about the risk of diseases, how to cope with them, what medicines to take, and how they affect people's lives. You are told about all of the vitamins and pills you need to consume to stay healthy. The same information is available for safety issues such as car accidents, accidents in the home and accidents with children.

Friends and family also contribute by talking about their own health problems and insisting that you too will experience the same problems as you get older. Focusing attention on this information and advice can create a pattern of thinking that illness and accidents are inevitable. Combine this with chronic daily negative thinking and it is almost impossible to stay safe and healthy.

You can choose your level of health and well-being everyday. When you are healthy, it is easier to focus on good health. Good health brings good thoughts about health. It is much easier to believe in good health and safety when there is no evidence to counter that belief. Yet when you are not well or you are fearful of bad health, it is harder to focus on good health. It is harder to let go, trust and allow.

When someone is in the midst of chemotherapy treatments, it is hard to believe unwaveringly that good health and wellness are possible and they can be achieved. But it can be done. The key is to not focus on what is staring you in the face. If you weigh more than you desire, if you are in pain, or if you have any unwanted condition, you must not focus on the weight, the pain or the condition. This might seem impossible since you take your body with you everywhere you go. But when you continue to observe what is wrong with your body, you continue to maintain your current condition.

Find a way to not focus on your body. Visualize yourself healthy, slimmer, disease-free, or pain-free. Imagine what you will look like. Put images and photos on your walls where you can give your attention. Think about things that feel good. Fantasize about what you will do when you achieve your thinner, healthier, or pain-free body. How will it feel to get up in the morning? How will it feel to move throughout the day? Use anything you can to distract yourself from the reality of today and focus on your desires for the future. The more you practice focusing on your desires, the easier it will be to distract yourself from the present and the sooner your desires will manifest.

You have to feel good now before you can achieve a state of feeling good later. Ignore what everyone else is telling you about your body and its prognosis. You know that you can be, do or have whatever your desire.

Your beliefs have a powerful impact on what happens to your body. You are taught certain "truths" about your body based on research and statistics. Remember, research and statistics reflect what is going on with someone else— not you. Truths are only beliefs that are repeated often, and beliefs are the result of repeated thoughts. What is true for someone else is not true for you.

What you believe is what you attract to your life. Some people believe—truly believe—that they can eat whatever they want, not exercise, and not gain weight. This is a truth for them. Others believe that if they just look at a piece of cake and run five miles, they will still gain weight. This is also a truth for them. Some people believe that they can drink and smoke every day and stay healthy. This is a truth for them. Others believe that their father died of a heart attack so they will as well. This, also, is a truth for them. You get what you believe.

Some will say they that they used to believe they could eat whatever they wanted and not gain weight, but then they started gaining weight. So, forces other than thoughts created their reality. The trick is that there is so much information from the media, doctors and friends that offer opinions on health. This information is so ingrained in your beliefs that it is hard to separate in your mind what you truly believe and what you have been told to believe.

How many times have you heard someone say or you thought to yourself, "*I really shouldn't eat this. It is not good for me*," and then they eat it? The person's belief about the food—not the food itself—makes it an unhealthy food to consume. Your beliefs guide your health, and you get what you think about.

You cannot become thin if you feel fat. Your focus is on being fat, and it creates resistance toward being thin. You might be able to lose some weight, but it will be a struggle, and you will probably eventually regain the weight. The same is true for smoking, drinking and other behaviors you want to stop. You have to visualize yourself as you want to be and allow this image to materialize. You will be as you see yourself. But be patient. If you have felt fat—or felt any unwanted condition—for thirty years, it will take time and practice to change your beliefs. They can, though, be changed. You get what you think about and believe.

Your body does not have to deteriorate as you age. It will if you believe it will, though. You do not have to get sick simply because every one in your home is sick. However, you will get sick if you believe you will get sick. Your beliefs are creating your reality. Chronic worry, anger, frustration and irritation create illness and accidents. Complaining about how your body looks or feels also keeps your body in its current state. You cannot improve when you are complaining about how you body is.

Change your thoughts about health while you are healthy and your health will be easier to maintain. If you have already manifested illness, don't worry. Just change your thoughts to reflect a more positive belief about your wellness. Practice thoughts of well-being. Practice positive thoughts and images about your body, and allow the natural good health that is your right to flow to you.

A state of joy is the greatest measure of success. Attaining a good-feeling body is one of the elements to sustaining a state of joy and wellness.

When you feel good, it is easier to feel joy and have a good attitude. Just as a good-feeling body promotes a positive attitude, a positive attitude promotes a good feeling body. When you do not feel good in your body, it affects all areas of your life. Your relationships, finances, career and lifestyle are all affected by your body's level of health. You take your body with you everywhere, so it can impact your experience with other things. This is why you need to feel good about your body. Your body is one of the easiest and fastest things to change in your experience.

Appreciate the positive aspects of your body. Appreciate what works in your body such as the dexterity of your fingers, the ability to breathe, the ability to sit, and the ability to think. Appreciate, appreciate, appreciate. Focus on what is good and ignore the rest.

Tell the story of how you want your body to look and feel. Imagine it. Talk about what you are doing with this new body. Spend fifteen minutes a day visualizing it and enjoying it. Trust in the process. Nothing is standing in the way between where you are now and where you want to be except for your own thoughts. You can change any condition in your body by changing your thought habits. When you get into the habit of thinking more positive thoughts, everything—including your body—will improve. You can feel better, look better and have more energy. Expect it and it is so.

Activity: Creating Your Health

It is difficult when you have a health condition that is not pleasing. The condition dominates your thoughts.

"I wish I didn't have this."
"I wish my body was like that person's."
"I don't feel well."
"I hurt."
"I'm scared."

The challenge to changing your health is to spend less time thinking about being unwell and more time thinking about your wellness. Your thoughts create your life, and if you can find a way to spend more time thinking about the wellness of your body and less time worrying or hating it, you will see a shift in how your body responds to you. Use some of the previous techniques to help you find better thoughts and feelings about your body.

- Use drawings to illustrate how you see yourself now and how you see yourself with the health problem resolved. Look for insight in those drawings.
- Use imagery to connect with how it feels to be in a body that is more pleasing.
- Use breathing techniques to calm your anxiety when you think about the problems of your body.
- Make a list or cut out pictures of all of the good things about your body and post these around your work and living space.
- Finally, commit to making a new small daily habit that will improve your health—maybe walk for fifteen minutes, drink more water, or meditate. When you find yourself doing this new thing effortlessly, then make another small change in your daily habit. Continue making small changes and you will discover big results.

A health condition is not a permanent state of being for your body. Your body is constantly changing and adapting to the environment. Take advantage how your body constantly evolves and create the health you desire.

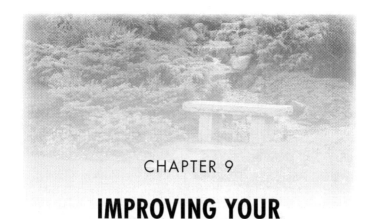

CHAPTER 9

IMPROVING YOUR RELATIONSHIPS

elationships are some of the most beautiful experiences to have, but they can also be some of the most frustrating and disappointing aspects of life. You will find that those around you will either admire your joyful life or they will go away. Other people's reactions however, do not have to impact you unless you choose to focus on them.

You cannot control the behavior and desires of others. No one can experience someone else's life and decide the best course of action for the other person. Your only true control is over your own thoughts and feelings and your ability to focus on what is pleasing to you. Another person will not affect you unless you allow it. Likewise, you don't need to control someone else in order to get something you want to happen.

Let others choose their own experiences. This world consists of contrast and diversity. The contrast is what helps you discern what you want and don't want in your life. Without contrast, you would not be able to identify your wants and then attract them. Others get to choose their own wants as well. Everyone has different experiences, so people are going to make different choices. People do what they believe is right for them—which often does not match what you believe to be right—and what they do is none of your business. Focus only on what you want and allow others to focus on what they want. Trust in other people's ability to lead their own lives. You don't have to save or fix anyone. In fact, you can't save or fix anyone. You don't have that kind of power. It's not your job to change the world for others; it's your job to change the world for yourself.

People often want to ask those around them to create a pleasing life for them. Expecting others to create a perfect world does not work because no one can create in another's life. A person would have to give up her own power in her life in order to allow someone else to affect her, and that creates an unhealthy relationship.

A common block in relationships is the belief, "I don't feel good, and I am blaming you for it. I don't feel good, and it's because of something you are doing." This comes from a feeling of powerlessness. One person will feel powerless to control his experience, and he will blame the person he believes has all of the power. Yet, one person cannot keep another feeling good. It is overwhelming and impossible. People have to figure out how to feel good on their own.

You, too, are responsible for your own feelings in a relationship. It does not matter if the person you are paying attention to is fun or annoying. You are in charge of your feelings, and you get to choose the feeling you feel at the moment in response to what you are observing. If you can't think positively toward the person to whom you are paying attention, then look the other way. Find something else more positive on which to focus. The choice is always yours.

You can't make others happy. The best gift you can give another is to create your own happiness. When you do what is right for you, all else will fall into place. You might be called selfish or self-centered because you insist on putting your happiness first and not giving into the demands of others. However, when you ignore your own desires and needs to please another, you are severely limiting your path to joy. You must meet your own needs first before being effective with another's needs.

When you are able to put your own feelings first and satisfy your need for happiness, you become a powerful force of light. You are so powerful that you know you control your own happiness and others control theirs. Feelings of hatred, judgment, resentment, or insecurity toward others have nothing to do with the targeted person or people. It is instead about the individual who feels these emotions, and that person must accept responsibility for improving her own experience. No one else can make her feel better except herself. As a powerful creator, you know this and it feels wonderful.

Parents often want to control their children. Ironically, children are still young enough to remember that they get to control their own lives. Children instinctively remember that they were born powerful beings, and they get to choose what is right for them. This conflicts with parents who amusingly believe that if they do not control their children, their children will naturally self-destruct. The battle is fought over who has control.

If the parents insist they are the one to choose for their children, the children will either give-up and accept the feeling of powerlessness, or they will rebel and react in rage. If children are not allowed to follow their own path, they are susceptible to repeating the unbalanced patterns they learned from their parents. They might engage in relationships where they feel powerless, or they might take their rage into other relationships. Teaching children to listen to their own emotions is the most powerful tool parents can give their children for living lives of joy and well-being.

Parents are obviously needed to guide their children as they grow and provide for their needs, but parents are not the only source for a child's wellness. Children can learn that they can be, do, or have whatever they desire. Children are creators, and this should be nurtured. Yet, children need to be taught that what they want does not only come through parents. Parents provide for much of their children's desires, but there are other avenues available for achieving their desires. Parents and children often get tangled in the dynamic of children wanting and parents denying. This creates much resentment and frustration between parents and children. You must empower your children to learn how to follow their own emotions and instincts to create their desires. If you try to meet every want of your child, you will be overwhelmed. Children who learn to ask and trust that their desires will be fulfilled through many avenues can learn to relax and enjoy all that life has to offer. Parents model how to live their own true path and how to listen to their feelings. This is the best gift to give children.

No one is ever wrong to feel a certain way. People's feelings are important indicators of where they are on their path. Feelings indicate whether they are pointed in the positive direction of wellness or if they are negatively focused. Let others feel what they feel. It is where they are, and where they need to be. You do not get to tell others that they need to feel differently than what they are feeling. Let them be. Be happy when someone feels anger. Anger feels better than depression, and you can wish for them the experience of feeling better than anger. Pay attention to what you feel when you are engaging with others, and move away if you are not able to provide a breath of relief to the situation.

Often, people listen to a news story or focus on a friend's problem in an effort to learn about what is happening, offer empathy and help. Yet, when you focus on another's problem and you feel bad, you are not helping their problem, and you may even attract the problem to yourself.

When you focus on something or someone and feel pain, you are only choosing to focus on the part of the person or situation that is negative. You are not looking at the whole person or situation. The pain you are experiencing is not from your empathy; it is from your own interpretation about what you are observing. You can also choose to focus on something good in the person or situation, and you will feel better. You can choose to see the whole person on a journey rather than focus on the moment of pain. You are more help to others if you can imagine a solution for their problems rather than joining them in their misery.

Friends, family and professionals are always ready and willing to offer advice on the choices you should make. Although their intentions are good, no one else has the ability to live your life and decide what feels good for you. No one else can decide the best path for you to follow or the best choice to make. Only you have access to your emotions, so only you know what feels good and what feels bad. You cannot get to where you want to be if you are listening to the advice and opinions of others. You can only follow one path—your own. You know the way that is right for you and what feels good.

Likewise, avoid comparing your life and experiences with those of others. Doing so can create a sense of lack in you if you feel you are not as good as the other. You don't need to compare yourself with anyone to see how you are doing. What anyone else is doing has nothing to do with you. What you are doing has nothing to do with anyone else. All you need to do is pay attention to your emotions to see how you are doing. If you are feeling better, then you are doing exactly what you need to.

Relationships are wonderful. Whether you are relating with someone in traffic or someone with whom you share your life, the moments can be magical. Allow others to live their lives and you live yours. Experience the beauty of relationships and feel good.

Activity: The List of Positive Qualities

Everyone has positive qualities, yet sometimes they are hard to see. Trust in the goodness of everyone—even if all you see is anger, destruction or hate. It might feel like a person has no goodness, but there is always something. Healers look at the whole person, and they can see people in their goodness. This view allows them to see people in their wellness and healing occurs. When you see the whole person and you see goodness, more positive qualities emerge.

Think about someone with whom you struggle to get along or like. Take paper and something with which to write, and write one good quality about that person. It could be something about the person's appearance, intelligence, ethics, contribution to society, or a nice comment that was shared. Think about that one positive quality and then write down others that come to mind. There are probably many negative qualities you could focus on as well, but keep your attention on the positive traits.

Continue doing this for about ten minutes. When you are finished, read through your list. How do you feel about this person now? Do you feel lighter? Does it seem easier to like this person? Are you feeling more positive?

Keep this list handy so you can add to it or read it the next time the person bothers you. You will find that the more you focus on the positive qualities, the less bothersome that person will appear.

The quality of relationship you have with someone is all about your ability to see the good things in that person and ignore the annoying ones. Keep in mind that people are doing the best they can with what they have in the moment. Be easy with others. Your relationships will blossom.

CHAPTER 10

FEELING GOOD ABOUT YOUR FINANCES

*M*oney is a tricky issue. It appears to be the road to happiness, yet many people with money are not happy. There is a common belief that with enough money, people can create the life of their dreams and live happily ever after. Yet happiness is not created through wealth—it is created by doing what feels right for you.

There are many people considered "poor" by society's standards who are living in bliss. Cultures throughout the world live their lives without restroom facilities, running water or solid housing. Yet many of these people live each day with joy, and they have no desire to change their financial situation. Likewise, many homes in more developed areas have every amenity needed for comfort yet these homes lack joy. Money does not bring joy, but it can open doors to many opportunities and adventures.

Decisions are often made based on what will bring more money or approval. These decisions rarely lead to joy. If you want to experience more money, then experience more joy first. You experience joy by doing what you love. Do what you love and the money will follow. There is no better way to earn money than doing what you love. There are others who say, "I can't believe I get paid to do this! I would do it for free!" It is possible to spend your days with work you enjoy while you earn the money you desire.

You might be struggling with the idea of finding a joyful career if you feel stuck in a "dead-end" job. You have to feel good where you are before you can allow something that you believe you will enjoy to enter your life. Find something to appreciate about your current job and focus on it. It might just be that you get to sit in a comfortable chair, that you are allowed to listen to music at work, or that you have a funny co-worker. Find something.

Once you find an aspect of your job that feels good, focus on it. You will still have some negative thoughts about where you are, but do not dwell on those. Return your focus to the one thing you can appreciate about your job. Eventually, you will discover a new opportunity for a career or a new, fun way to earn money. Your attitude about money—not the career you have chosen—is what brings money in or keeps it away.

Another way to increase the joy of your experience is to visualize your life as you want it to be with your finances. Spend time each day visualizing what your life will be like once you have all of the money you desire. See yourself writing the final checks to all of those institutions you owe money. As you write the checks, appreciate the institutions that loaned you the money when you needed it. Acknowledge that without these loans, you would not have been able to make your purchases or receive needed services. Imagine what fun things you will do with your new wealth. Where will you visit? What will you buy? What will feel good? Keep your thoughts focused on what feels good about having the money, and enjoy the visualization.

You do not have to figure out how the money is going to come to you. This will easily create a struggle. If you allow the money to flow, you will receive it.

Worrying about what will happen once you get the money will also create struggle. Anxiety about getting taxed, being robbed, being taken advantaged of, losing the money, and so on will stop the wealth before you see evidence of it. Trust that you will be provided with the resources and guidance needed to manage your desires.

Look at your beliefs about money. Society has a shared belief that money is evil, and those with money cannot be trusted.

- How comfortable are you with money?
- What are the messages you received regarding wealth?

- Did your parents spend their lives barely getting by?
- Did you experience lack while growing up?
- Are you working in a career that is low paying because you were taught that careers that pay a lot of money are consuming or bad?
- Do you believe that there are limited resources, and if you have more money than you need, others will have less?
- Do you believe money corrupts people?
- Do you believe money is evil?
- Is it wrong to want to be rich?

These experiences and thoughts become a part of your belief system and affect your relationship with money. Examine your beliefs about money. If you have negative thoughts tied to having money, or if you find yourself judging those with money—both their character and how they spend their money—then these thoughts can prevent your desires from manifesting. Many people do not want a lot of money, and they are fine where they are. Yet, if you do have a desire for greater wealth, then look at your current beliefs and practice new, positive thoughts.

Ultimately, money is not that big of a deal. Money does not guide your life. This might be hard to believe if you are staring at a looming foreclosure or if you have mounting medical bills. When these unfortunate experiences occur, they are accompanied by thoughts of worry and fear over money. When the situation gets worse, the feelings get worse, and hopelessness and despair surface, making the manifestation of more money even more of a challenge. Money is not that big of a deal because life is not about the money itself. Instead your beliefs about money and what you expect life to offer you create your experience. If you can't feel good about money, then don't think about it. Focus on thinking positive thoughts each day and have fun. This is really what life is meant to be.

Activity: Financial Ease

Consider the amount of debt you have. Does it seem like too much to manage? Does it seem hopeless? Remember, your perception of situations is what creates your feelings, and if you feel that something is hopeless, it is. Break down the bigger picture to find a manageable grasp on your financial issues. Handling your financial problems in smaller amounts is more feasible, and it just feels better.

You probably can't wipe out all of your debt this month, but you can do something to make a little reduction.

- Write down all of your debt, from the largest amount you owe (to the smallest.

- Make a commitment to pay a little more on your smallest debt this month. If you can pay double the minimum, great. If not, then just pay more than the minimum.

- As you pay your bill, take a deep breath and release the tension you feel about your finances. While you are practicing conscious breathing, say to yourself,

"I can't pay off all of my debt this month, but I can pay a little more to make it smaller."

- Don't think about how long this process will take. Just enjoy the empowering feeling that comes from knowing that you do have control managing your debt.

- State your appreciation for the businesses that lent you money so you could purchase the item or service you needed. Notice how good this feels.

- The amount of money you owe does not matter as much as the feeling you have about your debt. Feelings of panic and hopelessness will keep you stuck. Feelings of appreciation and hope will be inspiring.

- Don't think about your debt after you have paid the bills. Spend the rest of the month feeling good, and then when the next payments are due, pay a little more on your smallest debt than you did the previous month, and again appreciate the businesses that loaned you money when you needed it.

- Keep a record of your monthly accomplishments as you pay your bills. It might seem slow at first, but eventually you will build up enough momentum to see real financial changes occur.

These small steps will make a tremendous difference in your financial situation over time. It doesn't matter how small a change you make—just make a change. Real change happens in small steps, and small steps are easy to accomplish. You will feel better about your situation over time, and you will be able to allow bigger changes to happen. Trust in the process and let go of the worry. Make this a game, and let the fun begin.

CHAPTER 11

APPRECIATE

ppreciation is the absence of struggle, the absence of doubt and fear, the absence of self-denial and hatred, the absence of everything that feels bad. Appreciation is being immersed in all that feels good. Appreciation is seeing something or someone as *God* sees them. Appreciation allows you to focus on what is good and ignore what is bad. You can't appreciate and criticize at the same time. You can't see the annoying and irritating behaviors or habits when you appreciate someone. When you appreciate someone, you are seeing their spirit, and it feels good.

Appreciate all day long. Practice taking moments throughout the day and purposefully appreciate what you see. You could be stuck in traffic and appreciate that so many people are fortunate enough to have cars for transportation. You could be in the presence of someone who typically annoys you, but appreciate his dedication to his job. Appreciate the people in your life, your environment, your health, your government, your employment, your hobbies and your creature comforts.

Appreciation is the most powerful tool for improving the world. The government might be hard to appreciate because you might feel there are so many things wrong with those in power. Yet pushing against what you do not want only keeps you negatively focused, and it doesn't make much of a difference. When you truly appreciate all the government has to offer—education for all children, paved roads, utility and water service, nature preserves—you can begin to affect change more positively. Even if you can only find one thing about a person or thing to appreciate, use that one thing to make a difference. You are most powerful when you are appreciating because you are focused on something good. When you desire a change, turn your focus to appreciation and hold the person or thing in a light of wellness.

Appreciation opens you up and allows your desires to manifest. Since there is no struggle in appreciation, there is no resistance to your desires. Practicing appreciation is a powerful tool to affect change in your life. During the day, look for reasons to laugh and reasons to have fun. Create an environment where it is easy to feel good. Before going to sleep, give a few thoughts of appreciation to set the tone of your sleep. Think of the encounters you had during the day that you appreciated; acknowledge that you and your family have come together again at the end of the day.

Appreciate that you got to spend another day living your life and enjoying the people in your life, and appreciate this gift.

Appreciate all day—every day. Recognize the power of this activity. Put notes around your home and work place to remind you to appreciate. As you practice this each day, it will become more automatic. You will quickly see the benefits of appreciation. Your life will improve and you will feel good. This will give you even more to appreciate.

Activity: Appreciate! Appreciate! Appreciate!

This is an easy, yet powerful, activity. It is also one that is hard to remember to do. Any time you can choose to appreciate something rather than focus on the negative, you will be improving your life. When you are standing in line at the grocery store, when you are stuck in traffic, when you are trapped in a meeting, or when you are listening to your partner complain—these are the best times to appreciate. What do you appreciate? Whatever you can.

- The weather
- Something about your current health
- The architecture of buildings
- The people that came before you to create your world
- How easy it is to breathe, see, walk, talk, think
- The peace of your neighborhood
- Your pet
- Your kids

- Your spouse
- Chocolate cake
- Transportation
- A smile
- Holidays
- Music

The more you appreciate, the more you find to appreciate. You must be able to see the good in front of you before your world expands and brings you more things to appreciate. Choose to feel good because it feels good. You always have a choice about what you think, and choosing thoughts that feel good makes more sense than focusing on all that makes you feel bad. Even if you can only find a sliver of something to feel good about, focus on it! Soon, other things will reveal themselves to you that you can enjoy. Make the choice to appreciate. It feels good to feel good.

CHAPTER 12

WHERE TO GO FROM HERE

This is your chance to live the life you choose. It doesn't matter how much you accomplish as long as you feel good. The goal of life is freedom. Freedom is found in empowerment, and empowerment is found when you pay attention to your emotions. You get to choose what you feel, what you do, and how you live. The freedom of your life is breathtaking.

You have not been learning anything new in this course that you didn't already know. These ideas might resonate with you and you are hearing them in a new way. Look at the teachings of various religions, and you will find similar understandings and shared beliefs. Ultimately, trust yourself. You have all you need to live a joyful and successful life within you. No outside person or organization can guide you as clearly as you can guide yourself.

Be patient with the process. Do not tackle your biggest issue first—the one you have been struggling with for thirty years. The longer you have been trying to get rid of something unwanted, the longer it will take to shift your feelings concerning that issue. Many of your experiences are the result of years of negative thinking. It may take some time before you are able to adjust your pattern of thinking and practice offering more positive feelings. Begin with little changes you wish to make in your life. As you have success with the little changes, you will have the confidence to know that your bigger wants can be achieved. Practice feeling better by appreciating the current life you live and having an unwavering expectation that your dreams will evolve. When you find yourself looking at something that does not feel good, pivot and look at something that feels better. Your success in life is determined by how much joy you let yourself experience. Commit to focusing on positive thoughts and watch your life flood with your desires.

Expect good things. Know and believe that it is all possible. You can be, do or have anything you desire. Appreciate. Appreciate. Appreciate. All day and every day appreciate. Life is what happens as you journey toward your desires. The joy is on the journey. Once you accept that to be happy later you have to be happy now, you will then understand how to get all of your desires, and you can begin to relax and enjoy the journey.

Life is good. There is so much to experience and live. Enjoy your journey. You are here for a short time. Appreciate the experience of living during this time with those with whom you are sharing this journey. It is all good—really it is.

Activity: Dance! (Or at Least Move)*
Life experiences can cause our bodies to fill-up with energy or feelings that get stuck. This pent-up energy can cause us to feel overwhelmed and hopeless. Talking does not always release it. Physical activity, however, can be a great tool for resetting our system and balancing our energy.

Dancing is an easy way to get our feelings unstuck, raise our energy levels, and release tension. This is an activity to do by yourself where you are less likely to be self-conscious. The more you do it, the better you feel!

- Select a song that is upbeat and you enjoy.
- Find a room where you will be undisturbed while you dance.
- Don't worry about how you dance or what you look like. Just move your body.
- When you dance, initially keep your feet planted on the ground so you can stay more aware of your body movements.
- Keep your knees bent and your arms loose.
- Close your eyes if you can maintain your balance.
- Start the music and allow your body to loosely move to the rhythm.
- Notice how the movements of your legs, arms, and head flow to the music.

- Appreciate your heartbeat, your breathing, and your muscle responses.
- Keep pace with the rhythm of the music, focusing your thoughts only on the sounds.
- When the song ends, stand for a few moments and practice conscious breathing.
- Smile if you wish.

Dance a few minutes every day. This meditative activity of appreciation is a powerful tool for changing your life.

If you have health concerns, always check with your health care provider before attempting any physical activity.